Singapore MATH

MENTAL MATH
Strategies and Process Skills to Develop Mental Calculation

Grade 7
(Level 6)

Frank Schaffer
An imprint of Carson-Dellosa Publishing LLC
Greensboro, North Carolina

CREDITS

Content Editor: Karen Cermak-Serfass
Copy Editor: Barrie Hoople
Layout Design: Van Harris

This book has been correlated to state, common core state, national, and Canadian provincial standards. Visit www.carsondellosa.com to search for and view its correlations to your standards.

Copyright © 2011, Singapore Asian Publications (S) Pte Ltd

Frank Schaffer
An imprint of Carson-Dellosa Publishing LLC
PO Box 35665
Greensboro, NC 27425 USA

The purchase of this material entitles the buyer to reproduce worksheets and activities for classroom use only—not for commercial resale. Reproduction of these materials for an entire school or district is prohibited. No part of this book may be reproduced (except as noted above), stored in a retrieval system, or transmitted in any form or by any means (mechanically, electronically, recording, etc.) without the prior written consent of Carson-Dellosa Publishing LLC. Frank Schaffer is an imprint of Carson-Dellosa Publishing LLC.

Printed in the USA • All rights reserved.   ISBN 978-1-936024-13-1

ABOUT THIS BOOK

Welcome to Singapore Math! The national math curriculum used in Singapore has been recognized worldwide for its excellence in producing students highly skilled in mathematics. The country's students have ranked at the top in achievement in the world on the Trends in International Mathematics and Science Study (TIMSS) in 1993, 1995, 2003, and 2008. The study also shows that students in Singapore are typically one grade level ahead of students in the United States. Because of these trends, Singapore Math has gained interest and popularity.

Mathematics in the Singapore primary (elementary) curriculum covers fewer topics but in greater depth. Key math concepts are introduced and built upon to reinforce various mathematical ideas and thinking. Singapore Math curriculum aims to help students develop the necessary math process skills for everyday life and to provide students with the opportunity to master math concepts.

Mental Math Level 6, for grade 7, provides a comprehensive guide for mastering mental calculation. Each strategy in this book helps students perform mental calculation and obtain accurate answers in the shortest possible amount of time.

This book consists of 52 practice and review pages. Each practice page demonstrates a strategy with an example and includes 10 problems for students to solve. Students can then test their understanding by working on the review pages that are located after the practice pages.

To help students build and strengthen their mental calculation skills, this book provides strategies that will benefit students as they learn tips to solve math problems quickly and effectively. After acquiring such invaluable skills, students can apply them to their future, real-life experiences with math, such as in shopping and banking. *Mental Math Level 6* is an indispensable resource for all students who wish to master mental strategies and excel in them.

TABLE OF CONTENTS

	Strategies Overview	6
WEEK 1 STRATEGY	Adding a Series of Odd Numbers	8
WEEK 2 STRATEGY	Adding a Series of Even Numbers	9
WEEK 3 STRATEGY	Adding a Series of Consecutive Numbers	10
WEEK 4 STRATEGY	Adding a Series of Numbers in a Pattern	11
WEEK 5	**General Review 1**	12
WEEK 6 STRATEGY	Multiplying Numbers Ending with 9	13
WEEK 7 STRATEGY	Multiplying Numbers by 111	14
WEEK 8 STRATEGY	Multiplying Numbers by 125	15
WEEK 9 STRATEGY	Multiplying Five-Digit Numbers by 11	16
WEEK 10	**General Review 2**	17
WEEK 11 STRATEGY	Multiplying Consecutive Numbers from 90 to 100.............	18
WEEK 12 STRATEGY	Multiplying Consecutive Numbers from 100 to 110...........	19
WEEK 13 STRATEGY	Multiplying Whole Numbers by Mixed Numbers	20
WEEK 14 STRATEGY	Dividing Whole Numbers by Mixed Numbers	21
WEEK 15	**General Review 3**	22
WEEK 16 STRATEGY	Adding Three Special Fractions	23
WEEK 17 STRATEGY	Percentage: 2.5% of a Number	24
WEEK 18 STRATEGY	Percentage: 55% of a Number	25
WEEK 19 STRATEGY	Percentage: $33\frac{1}{3}$% of a Number	26
WEEK 20	**General Review 4**	27
WEEK 21 STRATEGY	Squaring Numbers from 50 to 90	28
WEEK 22 STRATEGY	Squaring Numbers from 100 to 109	29
WEEK 23 STRATEGY	Squaring: Adding the Square of a Number and its Double	30
WEEK 24 STRATEGY	Squaring: Subtracting the Squares of Two Consecutive Numbers	31
WEEK 25	**General Review 5**	32
WEEK 26 STRATEGY	Square Root: Finding the Square Root of Numbers Ending with 1	33

© Singapore Asian Publications (S) Pte Ltd

TABLE OF CONTENTS

WEEK 27 STRATEGY	Square Root: Finding the Square Root of Numbers Ending with 5	34
WEEK 28 STRATEGY	Cube Root: Finding the Cube Root of Numbers Ending with 2, 3, 7, and 8	35
WEEK 29 STRATEGY	Cube Root: Finding the Cube Root of Numbers Ending with 0, 1, 4, 5, 6, and 9	36
WEEK 30	General Review 6	37
WEEK 31 STRATEGY	Time: Finding the Day of the Week in the 21st Century	38
WEEK 32 STRATEGY	Time: Finding the Day of the Week in a 21st-Century Leap Year	39
WEEK 33 STRATEGY	Special Number 429	40
WEEK 34 STRATEGY	Special Number 715	41
WEEK 35	General Review 7	42
WEEK 36 STRATEGY	Special Number 858	43
WEEK 37 STRATEGY	Finding the Sum of Ascending Double Numbers	44
WEEK 38 STRATEGY	Finding the Sum of Ascending Triple Numbers	45
WEEK 39 STRATEGY	Finding the Product of any Number and 99	46
WEEK 40	General Review 8	47
WEEK 41	General Review 9	48
WEEK 42	General Review 10	49
WEEK 43	General Review 11	50
WEEK 44	General Review 12	51
WEEK 45	General Review 13	52
WEEK 46	General Review 14	53
WEEK 47	General Review 15	54
WEEK 48	General Review 16	55
WEEK 49	General Review 17	56
WEEK 50	General Review 18	57
WEEK 51	General Review 19	58
WEEK 52	General Review 20	59
ANSWER KEY		61

STRATEGIES OVERVIEW

The following overview provides examples of the various math problem types and skill sets taught in Singapore Math.

1 Adding a Series of Odd Numbers
$1 + 3 + 5 + 7 + 9 + 11 + 13 + 15 + 17 + 19 + 21 + 23 + 25 + 27 + 29 + 31 + 33 + 35 + 37 + 39 + 41 + 43 + 45$

$1 + 3 + 5 + \ldots + 45 \to 46$ Step 1: Find the next even number.
$46 \div 2 = 23$ Step 2: Divide the even number by 2.
$23 \times 23 = 529$ Step 3: Multiply the quotient obtained in Step 2 by itself.

$1 + 3 + 5 + 7 + 9 + 11 + \ldots + 45 = \mathbf{529}$

2 Adding a Series of Even Numbers
$2 + 4 + 6 + 8 + 10 + 12 + 14 + 16 + 18 + 20 + 22 + 24 + 26 + 28 + 30 + 32 + 34 + 36 + 38 + 40 + 42 + 44 + 46 + 48 + 50 + 52 + 54$

$54 \div 2 = 27$ Step 1: Divide the last number in the series by 2.
$27 + 1 = 28$ Step 2: Add 1 to the quotient obtained in Step 1.
$27 \times 28 = 756$ Step 3: Multiply the results obtained in Steps 1 and 2.

$2 + 4 + 6 + 8 + 10 + \ldots + 54 = \mathbf{756}$

3 Adding a Series of Consecutive Numbers
$16 + 17 + 18 + 19 + 20 + \ldots + 30$

$30 + 16 = 46$ Step 1: Find the sum of the last and first numbers in the series.
$30 - 16 = 14$ Step 2: Find the difference of the last and first numbers in the series.
$14 + 1 = 15$ Step 3: Add 1 to the difference obtained in Step 2.
$(46 \times 15) \div 2 = 690 \div 2 = 345$ Step 4: Find the product of the sums obtained in Steps 1 and 3. Divide the product by 2 to find the answer.

$16 + 17 + 18 + 19 + 20 + \ldots + 30 = \mathbf{345}$

4 Adding a Series of Numbers in a Pattern
$8 + 10 + 12 + 14 + 16 + 18 + 20$

$8 + 10 + 12 + \mathbf{14} + 16 + 18 + 20$ Step 1: Find the middle number in the pattern. For this number series, it is 14.
$\;\;1\;\;\;2\;\;\;3\;\;\;4\;\;\;5\;\;\;6\;\;\;7$
$8 + 10 + 12 + 14 + 16 + 18 + 20$ Step 2: Count the total number of addends. For this number series, it is 7.
$14 \times 7 = 98$ Step 3: Find the product of the results obtained in Steps 1 and 2.

$8 + 10 + 12 + 14 + 16 + 18 + 20 = \mathbf{98}$

6 Multiplying Numbers Ending with 9
59×89
$(50 + 9) \times (80 + 9)$ Step 1: Expand both factors.
$50 \times 80 = 4{,}000$ Step 2: Find the product of the tens.
$(50 \times 9) + (80 \times 9) = 450 + 720 = 1{,}170$ Step 3: Multiply the tens and the ones of each factor. Find the sum of the products.
$(4{,}000 + 1{,}170) + 81 = 5{,}170 + 81 = 5{,}251$ Step 4: Add the results obtained in Steps 2 and 3. Then, add 81 to find the answer.

$59 \times 89 = \mathbf{5{,}251}$

7 Multiplying Numbers by 111
58×111
$58 \times 100 = 5{,}800$ Step 1: Multiply the first factor by 100.
$58 \times 11 = (50 \times 11) + (8 \times 11)$
$= 550 + 88$
$= 638$ Step 2: Expand the factor. Multiply both parts by 11.
$5{,}800 + 638 = 6{,}438$ Step 3: Find the sum of the products obtained in Steps 1 and 2.

$58 \times 111 = \mathbf{6{,}438}$

8 Multiplying Numbers by 125
88×125
$(88 \div 8) \times 1{,}000$ Step 1: Divide the first factor by 8.
$= 11 \times 1{,}000$
$= 11{,}000$ Step 2: Multiply the quotient obtained in Step 1 by 1,000.

$88 \times 125 = \mathbf{11{,}000}$

9 Multiplying Five-Digit Numbers by 11
$74{,}269 \times 11$
$(74{,}269 \times 10) + 74{,}269$ Step 1: Multiply the five-digit factor by 10.
$= 742{,}690 + 74{,}269$
$= 816{,}959$ Step 2: Add the five-digit factor to the product obtained in Step 1.

$74{,}269 \times 11 = \mathbf{816{,}959}$

11 Multiplying Consecutive Numbers from 90 to 100
90×91
Step 1: $100 - 91 = 9$ ❑ Subtract the greater factor from 100.
Step 2: To find the last two digits of the answer,
$9 \times (9 + 1)$ ❑ Multiply the difference by the number one greater than itself.
$= 9 \times 10$
$= 90$
Step 3: To find the first few digits of the answer,
$90 - 9 = 81$ ❑ Subtract the difference obtained in Step 1 from the smaller factor.
$90 \times 91 = \mathbf{8{,}190}$

12 Multiplying Consecutive from 100 to 110
105×106
Step 1: $105 - 100 = 5$ ❑ Subtract 100 from the smaller factor.
Step 2: To find the last two digits of the answer,
$5 \times (5 + 1)$ ❑ Multiply the difference by the number one greater than itself.
$= 5 \times 6$
$= 30$
Step 3: To find the first few digits of the answer,
$106 + 5 = 111$ ❑ Add the difference obtained in Step 1 to the greater factor.
$105 \times 106 = \mathbf{11{,}130}$

13 Multiplying Whole Numbers by Mixed Numbers
$50 \times 1\frac{1}{6}$

$\frac{50}{1} \times \frac{1}{6} = \frac{50}{6}$ Step 1: Multiply the whole number by the fraction in the mixed number.
$\frac{50}{6} = 8\frac{1}{3}$ Step 2: Find the mixed number of the fraction obtained in Step 1.
$8\frac{1}{3} + 50 = 58\frac{1}{3}$ Step 3: Add the mixed number obtained in Step 2 to the original whole number.

$50 \times 1\frac{1}{6} = \mathbf{58\frac{1}{3}}$

14 Dividing Whole Numbers by Mixed Numbers
$25 \div 1\frac{1}{4}$

$1\frac{1}{4} = \frac{5}{4}$ Step 1: Convert the mixed number to an improper fraction.
$25 \div 5 = 5$ Step 2: Divide the whole number by the numerator of the improper fraction.
$5 \times 4 = 20$ Step 3: Multiply the quotient obtained in Step 2 by the denominator of the improper fraction.

$25 \div 1\frac{1}{4} = \mathbf{20}$

16 Adding Three Special Fractions
$\frac{1}{20} + \frac{1}{30} + \frac{1}{42}$

$\frac{1}{20} + \frac{1}{30} + \frac{1}{42} =$
$(4 \times 5)\;(5 \times 6)\;(6 \times 7)$ Step 1: Be sure that the factors of the denominators are consecutive.
$4, 5, 6, 7$
$4 \times 7 = \mathbf{28}$ Step 2: Find the product of the smallest and greatest factors. The product is the denominator of the answer.
$\frac{1 + 1 + 1}{28} = \frac{3}{28}$ Step 3: Add all three numerators. The sum is the numerator of the answer.

17 Percentage: 2.5% of a Number
Find the value of 2.5% of 60.
$60 \div 2 = 30$ Step 1: Divide the number by 2.
$30 \div 2 = 15$ Step 2: Divide the quotient obtained in Step 1 by 2.
$15 \div 10 = 1.5$ Step 3: Divide the quotient obtained in Step 2 by 10.
$2.5\% \times 60 = \mathbf{1.5}$

18 Percentage: 55% of a Number
Find the value of 55% of 50.
$50 \div 2 = 25$ Step 1: Divide the number by 2.
$25 \times 11 = 275$ Step 2: Multiply the quotient obtained in Step 1 by 11.
$275 \div 10 = 27.5$ Step 3: Divide the product obtained in Step 2 by 10.
55% of $50 = \mathbf{27.5}$

19 Percentage: $33\frac{1}{3}\%$ of a Number
Find the value of $33\frac{1}{3}\%$ of 120.
$120 \div 3 = 40$ ❑ Divide the whole number by the denominator.
$33\frac{1}{3}\%$ of $120 = \mathbf{40}$

21 Squaring Numbers from 50 to 90
66^2
Step 1: To find the last digit of the answer,
$6^2 = 3\underline{6}$ ❑ Square the ones digit of the number. Carry the tens digit from the result to the next step.
Step 2: To find the next-to-last-digit of the answer,
$(6 \times 6) \times 2$
$= 36 \times 2$
$= 72 + 3$
$= 7\underline{5}$ ❑ Multiply the ones and the tens digits of the number by 2.
   ❑ Add the digit carried from Step 1. Carry the tens digit from the result to the next step.
Step 3: To find the first few digits of the answer,
$6^2 = 36$ ❑ Square the tens digit of the number. Add the digit carried from Step 2.
$36 + 7 = \underline{43}$
$66^2 = \mathbf{4{,}356}$

22 Squaring Numbers from 100 to 109
102^2
Step 1: To find the last two digits of the answer,
$2^2 = 4$ ☐ Square the ones digit of the number.
If the result of Step 1 is a one-digit number, put a 0 in the tens place.
Step 2: To find the first few digits of the answer,
$(2 \times 2) + 100$ ☐ Multiply the ones digit of the number by 2.
$= 4 + 100$ Add 100 to the product to find the answer.
$= 104$
$102^2 = 10,404$

23 Squaring: Adding the Square of a Number and its Double
$7^2 + 14^2$
$7 + 7 = 14$ Step 1: Be sure that the larger addend is a double of the smaller addend.
$7^2 = 49$ Step 2: Square the smaller addend.
$49 \times 5 = 245$ Step 3: Multiply the result by 5 to find the answer.
$7^2 + 14^2 = 245$

24 Squaring: Subtracting the Squares of Two Consecutive Numbers
$11^2 - 10^2$
$10 + 0.5 = 10.5$ Step 1: Add 0.5 to the smaller number.
$10.5 \times 2 = 21$ Step 2: Multiply the result by 2 to find the answer.
$11^2 - 10^2 = 21$

26 Square Root: Finding the Square Root of Numbers Ending with 1
$\sqrt{6,561}$
Step 1: To find the first digit of the answer,
$\sqrt{65} \approx \sqrt{64} = \mathbf{8}^2$ ☐ Use the first two digits in the number to determine the closest lower square root whole number.
Note: If the number has three digits, determine the closest square root whole number of the first digit.
If the number has five digits, determine the closest square root whole number of the first three digits.
Step 2: The last digit of the answer is always 1.
$\sqrt{6,561} = 81$

27 Square Root: Finding the Square Root of Numbers Ending with 5
$\sqrt{2,025}$
Step 1: To find the first digit of the answer,
$\sqrt{20} \approx \sqrt{16} = \mathbf{4}^2$ ☐ Use the first two digits in the number to determine the closest lower square root whole number.
Note: If the number has three digits, determine the closest square root whole number of the first digit.
If the number has five digits, determine the closest square root whole number of the first three digits.
Step 2: The last digit of the answer is always 5.
$\sqrt{2,025} = 45$

28 Cube Root: Finding the Cube Root of Numbers Ending with 2, 3, 7, and 8
$\sqrt[3]{2,197}$
Step 1: To find the first digit of the answer,
$\sqrt[3]{2} \approx \sqrt[3]{1} = \mathbf{1}^3$ ☐ Use the thousands place value digit in the number to determine the closest lower cube root whole number.
Note: If the number has five digits, determine the closest cube root whole number of the first two digits.

last digit of the number	last digit of the answer
2	8
3	7
7	3
8	2

Step 2: Refer to the table to find the last digit of the answer.

$\sqrt[3]{2,197} = 13$

29 Cube Root: Finding the Cube Root of Numbers Ending with 0, 1, 4, 5, 6, and 9
$\sqrt[3]{13,824}$
Step 1: To find the first digit of the answer,
$\sqrt[3]{13} \approx \sqrt[3]{8} = \mathbf{2}^3$ ☐ Use the first two digits in the number to determine the closest lower cube root whole number.
Step 2: The last digit of the number will be the last digit of the answer.
$\sqrt[3]{13,824} = 24$

31 Time: Finding the Day of the Week in the 21st Century
Find the day of the week for June 6, 2007.
$1\frac{1}{4} \times 07 = \frac{5}{4} \times 7$ Step 1: Multiply the last two digits of the year by $1\frac{1}{4}$. The whole number is the year calculation.
$= \frac{35}{4} = 8\frac{3}{4}$

$8 + 3 + 6 = 17$ Step 2: Find the sum of the year calculation, the month code, and the date day: Year calculation = 8 (whole number from Step 1); Month code = 3 (Refer to the table.); Date day = 6.

January	6	July	5
February	2	August	1
March	2	September	4
April	5	October	6
May	0	November	2
June	3	December	4

$17 \div 7 = 2$ **R3** Step 3: Divide the sum obtained in Step 2 by 7.
Sunday = 0
Monday = 1 Step 4: Find the remainder from Step 3 in the list to find the day of the week. Since the remainder is 3, the day of the week is Wednesday.
Tuesday = 2
Wednesday = 3 ...

32 Time: Finding the Day of the Week in a 21st-Century Leap Year
Find the day of the week for February 12, 2004 (a leap year).
$1\frac{1}{4} \times 04 = \frac{5}{4} \times 4$ Step 1: Multiply the last two digits of the year by $1\frac{1}{4}$. The result is the year calculation.
$= \frac{20}{4} = 5$

$5 + 2 + 12 = 19$ Step 2: Find the sum of the year calculation, the month code, and the date day: Year calculation = 5 (whole number from Step 1); Month code = 2 (Refer to the table); Date day = 12.

January	6	July	5
February	2	August	1
March	2	September	4
April	5	October	6
May	0	November	2
June	3	December	4

$19 - 1 = 18$
$18 \div 7 = 2$ **R4** Step 3: If the month of the date falls in January or February, subtract 1 from the sum obtained in Step 2. Divide the result by 7.
Sunday = 0
Monday = 1
Tuesday = 2 Step 4: Find the remainder from Step 3 in the list to find the day of the week. Since the remainder is 4, the day of the week is Thursday.
Wednesday = 3
Thursday = 4 ...

33 Special Number 429
35×429
$35 \times \frac{3}{7} = \frac{105}{7}$ Step 1: Multiply the first factor by $\frac{3}{7}$.
$= 15$
015 Step 2: Put a 0 before the product obtained in Step 1 to establish the hundreds place.
$35 \times 429 = 15,015$ Step 3: Starting with the ten thousands place, combine the results obtained in Steps 1 and 2.

Note: This strategy only works if the number multiplied by 429 is a multiple of 7.

34 Special Number 715
42×715
$42 \times \frac{5}{7} = \frac{210}{7}$ Step 1: Multiply the first factor by $\frac{5}{7}$.
$= 30$
030 Step 2: Put a 0 before the product obtained in Step 1 to establish the hundreds place.
$42 \times 715 = 30,030$ Step 3: Starting with the ten thousands place, combine the results obtained in Steps 1 and 2.

Note: This strategy only works if the number multiplied by 715 is a multiple of 7.

36 Special Number 858
63×858
$63 \times \frac{6}{7} = \frac{378}{7}$ Step 1: Multiply the first factor by $\frac{6}{7}$.
$= 54$
054 Step 2: Put a 0 before the product obtained in Step 1 to establish the hundreds place.
$63 \times 858 = 54,054$ Step 3: Starting with the ten thousands place, combine the results obtained in Steps 1 and 2.

Note: This strategy only works if the number multiplied by 858 is a multiple of 7.

37 Finding the Sum of Ascending Double Numbers
$5 + 10 + 20 + 40 + 80$
Step 1: Be sure that each number in the series is twice the preceding number.
$80 \times 2 = 160$ Step 2: Multiply the largest addend by 2.
$160 - 5 = 155$ Step 3: Subtract the smallest addend from the product obtained in Step 2.
$5 + 10 + 20 + 40 + 80 = 155$

38 Finding the Sum of Ascending Triple Numbers
$2 + 6 + 18 + 54$
Step 1: Be sure that each number in the series is three times the preceding number.
$54 \times 3 = 162$ Step 2: Multiply the largest addend by 3.
$162 - 2 = 160$ Step 3: Subtract the smallest addend from the product obtained in Step 2.
$160 \div 2 = 80$ Step 4: Divide the difference obtained in Step 3 by 2.
$2 + 6 + 18 + 54 = 80$

39 Finding the Product of any Number and 99
123×99
$123 \times 100 = 12,300$ Step 1: Multiply the first factor by 100.
$12,300 - 123 = 12,177$ Step 2: Subtract the first factor from the product obtained in Step 1.
$123 \times 99 = 12,177$

WEEK 1

STRATEGY

Adding a Series of Odd Numbers

Strategy

Find the value of 1 + 3 + 5 + 7 + 9 + 11 + 13 + 15 + 17 + 19 + 21 + 23 + 25 + 27 + 29 + 31 + 33 + 35 + 37 + 39 + 41 + 43 + 45.

1 + 3 + 5 + ... + 45 → 46   Step 1: Find the next even number.
46 ÷ 2 = 23   Step 2: Divide the even number by 2.
23 × 23 = 529   Step 3: Multiply the quotient obtained in Step 2 by itself.

1 + 3 + 5 + 7 + 9 + 11 + ... + 45 = **529**

Solve each problem mentally.

1. 1 + 3 + 5 + 7 + 9 + 11 + ... + 39 =   400
2. 1 + 3 + 5 + 7 + 9 + 11 + ... + 17 =   81
3. 1 + 3 + 5 + 7 + 9 + 11 + ... + 53 =   729
4. 1 + 3 + 5 + 7 + 9 + 11 + ... + 47 =   576
5. 1 + 3 + 5 + 7 + 9 + 11 + ... + 25 =   169
6. 1 + 3 + 5 + 7 + 9 + 11 + ... + 81 =   1681
7. 1 + 3 + 5 + 7 + 9 + 11 + ... + 79 =   1600
8. 1 + 3 + 5 + 7 + 9 + 11 + ... + 65 =   1089
9. 1 + 3 + 5 + 7 + 9 + 11 + ... + 93 =   2209
10. 1 + 3 + 5 + 7 + 9 + 11 + ... + 29 =   225

STRATEGY

Adding a Series of Even Numbers

Strategy

Find the value of 2 + 4 + 6 + 8 + 10 + 12 + 14 + 16 + 18 + 20 + 22 + 24 + 26 + 28 + 30 + 32 + 34 + 36 + 38 + 40 + 42 + 44 + 46 + 48 + 50 + 52 + 54.

54 ÷ 2 = 27   Step 1: Divide the last number in the series by 2.
27 + 1 = 28   Step 2: Add 1 to the quotient obtained in Step 1.
27 × 28 = 756 Step 3: Multiply the results obtained in Steps 1 and 2.

2 + 4 + 6 + 8 + 10 + ... + 54 = **756**

Solve each problem mentally.

1. 2 + 4 + 6 + 8 + 10 + ... + 86 = 1892
2. 2 + 4 + 6 + 8 + 10 + ... + 98 = 2450
3. 2 + 4 + 6 + 8 + 10 + ... + 26 = 182
4. 2 + 4 + 6 + 8 + 10 + ... + 44 = 506
5. 2 + 4 + 6 + 8 + 10 + ... + 66 = 1122
6. 2 + 4 + 6 + 8 + 10 + ... + 50 = 650
7. 2 + 4 + 6 + 8 + 10 + ... + 32 = 272
8. 2 + 4 + 6 + 8 + 10 + ... + 74 = 1406
9. 2 + 4 + 6 + 8 + 10 + ... + 18 = 90
10. 2 + 4 + 6 + 8 + 10 + ... + 52 = 602

WEEK 3

STRATEGY

Adding a Series of Consecutive Numbers

Strategy

Find the value of 16 + 17 + 18 + 19 + 20 + ... + 30.

30 + 16 = 46	Step 1: Find the sum of the last and first numbers in the series.
30 − 16 = 14	Step 2: Find the difference of the last and first numbers in the series.
14 + 1 = 15	Step 3: Add 1 to the difference obtained in Step 2.
(46 × 15) ÷ 2 = 690 ÷ 2 = 345	Step 4: Find the product of the sums obtained in Steps 1 and 3. Divide the product by 2 to find the answer.

16 + 17 + 18 + 19 + 20 + . . . + 30 = **345**

Solve each problem mentally.

1. 10 + 11 + 12 + 13 + 14 + ... + 80 =   3195
2. 15 + 16 + 17 + 18 + 19 + ... + 40 =   1,430
3. 30 + 31 + 32 + 33 + 34 + ... + 60 =   2790
4. 32 + 33 + 34 + 35 + 36 + ... + 50 =   3,198
5. 45 + 46 + 47 + 48 + 49 + ... + 80 =   4,500
6. 19 + 20 + 21 + 22 + 23 + ... + 60 =   1654
7. 40 + 41 + 42 + 43 + 44 + ... + 70 =   1705
8. 25 + 26 + 27 + 28 + 29 + ... + 80 =   5180
9. 12 + 13 + 14 + 15 + 16 + ... + 50 =   1,209
10. 16 + 17 + 18 + 19 + 20 + ... + 90 =   3975

WEEK 4

STRATEGY

Adding a Series of Numbers in a Pattern

Strategy

Find the value of 8 + 10 + 12 + 14 + 16 + 18 + 20.

8 + 10 + 12 + **14** + 16 + 18 + 20

 1   2   3   4   5   6   7
8 + 10 + 12 + 14 + 16 + 18 + 20

14 × 7 = 98

8 + 10 + 12 + 14 + 16 + 18 + 20 = **98**

Step 1: Find the middle number in the pattern. For this number series, it is 14.

Step 2: Count the total number of addends. For this number series, it is 7.

Step 3: Find the product of the results obtained in Steps 1 and 2.

Solve each problem mentally.

1. 20 + 22 + 24 + 26 + 28 =
2. 14 + 16 + 18 + 20 + 22 =
3. 35 + 37 + 39 + 41 + 43 =
4. 59 + 61 + 63 + 65 + 67 =
5. 47 + 49 + 51 + 53 + 55 + 57 + 59 =
6. 66 + 68 + 70 + 72 + 74 + 76 + 78 =
7. 100 + 102 + 104 + 106 + 108 + 110 + 112 =
8. 148 + 150 + 152 + 154 + 156 + 158 + 160 =
9. 70 + 72 + 74 + 76 + 78 + 80 + 82 + 84 + 86 =
10. 190 + 192 + 194 + 196 + 198 + 200 + 202 + 204 + 206 =

GENERAL REVIEW 1

Solve each problem mentally.

1. 1 + 3 + 5 + 7 + 9 + 11 + ... + 99 =

2. 2 + 4 + 6 + 8 + 10 + ... + 40 =

3. 15 + 16 + 17 + 18 + 19 + ... + 60 =

4. 72 + 74 + 76 + 78 + 80 =

5. 2 + 4 + 6 + 8 + 10 + ... + 34 =

6. 38 + 39 + 40 + 41 + 42 + ... + 60 =

7. 120 + 122 + 124 + 126 + 128 + 130 + 132 =

8. 86 + 88 + 90 + 92 + 94 + 96 + 98 + 100 + 102 =

9. 1 + 3 + 5 + 7 + 9 + 11 + ... + 119 =

10. 27 + 28 + 29 + 30 + 31 + ... + 80 =

© Singapore Asian Publications (S) Pte Ltd

STRATEGY

Multiplying Numbers Ending with 9

Strategy

Find the value of 59 × 89.

(50 + 9) × (80 + 9)
50 × 80 = 4,000
(50 × 9) + (80 × 9)
= 450 + 720
= 1,170
(4,000 + 1,170) + 81
= 5,170 + 81
= 5,251

59 × 89 = **5,251**

Step 1: Expand both factors.
Step 2: Find the product of the tens.
Step 3: Multiply the tens and the ones of each factor. Find the sum of the products.
Step 4: Add the results obtained in Steps 2 and 3. Then, add 81 to find the answer.

Solve each problem mentally.

1. 49 × 29 =
2. 29 × 39 =
3. 69 × 49 =
4. 59 × 19 =
5. 89 × 69 =
6. 39 × 79 =
7. 79 × 89 =
8. 99 × 99 =
9. 19 × 49 =
10. 99 × 39 =

WEEK 1 STRATEGY

Multiplying Numbers by 111

Strategy

Find the value of 58 × 111.

58 × 100 = 5,800 Step 1: Multiply the first factor by 100.

58 × 11 = (50 × 11) + (8 × 11) Step 2: Expand the factor. Multiply both
       = 550 + 88   parts by 11.
       = 638

5,800 + 638 = 6,438 Step 3: Find the sum of the products obtained in Steps 1 and 2.

58 × 111 = **6,438**

Solve each problem mentally.

1. 22 × 111 =
2. 46 × 111 =
3. 39 × 111 =
4. 64 × 111 =
5. 90 × 111 =
6. 72 × 111 =
7. 55 × 111 =
8. 81 × 111 =
9. 79 × 111 =
10. 17 × 111 =

STRATEGY

Multiplying Numbers by 125

Strategy

Find the value of 88 × 125.

(88 ÷ 8) × 1,000
= 11 × 1,000
= 11,000

88 × 125 = **11,000**

Step 1: Divide the first factor by 8.
Step 2: Multiply the quotient obtained in Step 1 by 1,000.

Solve each problem mentally.

1. 72 × 125 =
2. 84 × 125 =
3. 48 × 125 =
4. 56 × 125 =
5. 64 × 125 =
6. 96 × 125 =
7. 28 × 125 =
8. 52 × 125 =
9. 16 × 125 =
10. 40 × 125 =

WEEK 9

STRATEGY

Multiplying Five-Digit Numbers by 11

Strategy

Find the value of 74,269 × 11.

(74,269 × 10) + 74,269
= 742,690 + 74,269
= 816,959

Step 1: Multiply the five-digit factor by 10.
Step 2: Add the five-digit factor to the product obtained in Step 1.

74,269 × 11 = **816,959**

Solve each problem mentally.

1. 41,036 × 11 =
2. 81,433 × 11 =
3. 92,698 × 11 =
4. 56,244 × 11 =
5. 18,417 × 11 =
6. 34,699 × 11 =
7. 61,852 × 11 =
8. 73,218 × 11 =
9. 24,167 × 11 =
10. 50,379 × 11 =

WEEK 10

GENERAL REVIEW 2

Solve each problem mentally.

1. 59 × 99 =

2. 44 × 111 =

3. 79 × 79 =

4. 29 × 89 =

5. 37 × 111 =

6. 42,936 × 11 =

7. 68 × 125 =

8. 36,127 × 11 =

9. 20 × 125 =

10. 24,197 × 11 =

WEEK 11

STRATEGY

Multiplying Consecutive Numbers from 90 to 100

Strategy

Find the value of 90 × 91.

Step 1: 100 − 91 = 9   ❏ Subtract the greater factor from 100.

Step 2: To find the last two digits of the answer,

9 × (9 + 1)   ❏ Multiply the difference by the number
= 9 × 10   one greater than itself.
= **90**

Step 3: To find the first few digits of the answer,

90 − 9 = **81**   ❏ Subtract the difference obtained in Step 1 from the smaller factor.

90 × 91 = **8,190**

Note: If Step 2 results in a one-digit number, put a 0 in the tens place.

Solve each problem mentally.

1. 93 × 94 =
2. 98 × 99 =
3. 95 × 96 =
4. 91 × 92 =
5. 97 × 98 =
6. 94 × 95 =
7. 92 × 93 =
8. 99 × 100 =
9. 96 × 97 =
10. 90 × 91 =

WEEK 12

STRATEGY

Multiplying Consecutive Numbers from 100 to 110

Strategy

Find the value of 105 × 106.

Step 1: 105 − 100 = 5 ❑ Subtract 100 from the smaller factor.

Step 2: To find the last two digits of the answer,

5 × (5 + 1)
= 5 × 6
= **30**

❑ Multiply the difference by the number one greater than itself.

Step 3: To find the first few digits of the answer,

106 + 5 = **111** ❑ Add the difference obtained in Step 1 to the greater factor.

105 × 106 = **11,130**

Solve each problem mentally.

1. 104 × 105 =
2. 106 × 107 =
3. 101 × 102 =
4. 107 × 108 =
5. 103 × 104 =
6. 100 × 101 =
7. 109 × 110 =
8. 102 × 103 =
9. 108 × 109 =
10. 105 × 106 =

WEEK 13

STRATEGY

Multiplying Whole Numbers by Mixed Numbers

Strategy

Find the value of $50 \times 1\frac{1}{6}$.

$\frac{50}{1} \times \frac{1}{6} = \frac{50}{6}$

$\frac{50}{6} = 8\frac{1}{3}$

$8\frac{1}{3} + 50 = 58\frac{1}{3}$

$50 \times 1\frac{1}{6} = \mathbf{58\frac{1}{3}}$

Step 1: Multiply the whole number by the fraction in the mixed number.
Step 2: Find the mixed number of the fraction obtained in Step 1.
Step 3: Add the mixed number obtained in Step 2 to the original whole number.

Note: This strategy only works when the whole number and the numerator of the mixed number are 1.

Solve each problem mentally.

1. $30 \times 1\frac{1}{3} =$
2. $29 \times 1\frac{1}{5} =$
3. $49 \times 1\frac{1}{7} =$
4. $21 \times 1\frac{1}{4} =$
5. $90 \times 1\frac{1}{6} =$
6. $73 \times 1\frac{1}{2} =$
7. $55 \times 1\frac{1}{9} =$
8. $60 \times 1\frac{1}{10} =$
9. $84 \times 1\frac{1}{5} =$
10. $99 \times 1\frac{1}{3} =$

WEEK 14

STRATEGY

Dividing Whole Numbers by Mixed Numbers

Strategy

Find the value of $25 \div 1\frac{1}{4}$.

$1\frac{1}{4} = \frac{5}{4}$ Step 1: Convert the mixed number to an improper fraction.

$25 \div 5 = 5$ Step 2: Divide the whole number by the numerator of the improper fraction.

$5 \times 4 = 20$ Step 3: Multiply the quotient obtained in Step 2 by the denominator of the improper fraction.

$25 \div 1\frac{1}{4} = \mathbf{20}$

Note: This strategy only works when the whole number and the numerator of the mixed number are 1.

Solve each problem mentally.

1. $24 \div 1\frac{1}{7} =$
2. $36 \div 1\frac{1}{3} =$
3. $42 \div 1\frac{1}{6} =$
4. $54 \div 1\frac{1}{5} =$
5. $70 \div 1\frac{1}{9} =$
6. $80 \div 1\frac{1}{4} =$
7. $39 \div 1\frac{1}{2} =$
8. $81 \div 1\frac{1}{8} =$
9. $90 \div 1\frac{1}{5} =$
10. $84 \div 1\frac{1}{6} =$

WEEK 15

GENERAL REVIEW 3

Solve each problem mentally.

1. 107 × 108 =

2. 16 × 1 $\frac{1}{7}$ =

3. 94 × 95 =

4. 95 ÷ 1 $\frac{1}{4}$ =

5. 54 × 1 $\frac{1}{3}$ =

6. 78 ÷ 1 $\frac{1}{5}$ =

7. 20 ÷ 1 $\frac{1}{3}$ =

8. 80 × 1 $\frac{1}{2}$ =

9. 91 × 92 =

10. 106 × 107 =

WEEK 16

STRATEGY

Adding Three Special Fractions

Strategy

Find the value of $\frac{1}{20} + \frac{1}{30} + \frac{1}{42}$.

$\frac{1}{20} + \frac{1}{30} + \frac{1}{42} =$
$(4 \times 5)\ (5 \times 6)\ (6 \times 7)$

4, 5, 6, **7**

$4 \times 7 = \mathbf{28}$

$\frac{1 + 1 + 1}{28} = \frac{\mathbf{3}}{\mathbf{28}}$

Step 1: Be sure that the factors of the denominators are consecutive.

Step 2: Find the product of the smallest and greatest factors. The product is the denominator of the answer.

Step 3: Add all three numerators. The sum is the numerator of the answer.

Note: This strategy only works with addend fractions that have 1 as the numerator.

Solve each problem mentally. Do not simplify to lowest terms.

1. $\frac{1}{6} + \frac{1}{12} + \frac{1}{20} =$

2. $\frac{1}{30} + \frac{1}{42} + \frac{1}{56} =$

3. $\frac{1}{156} + \frac{1}{182} + \frac{1}{210} =$

4. $\frac{1}{72} + \frac{1}{90} + \frac{1}{110} =$

5. $\frac{1}{42} + \frac{1}{56} + \frac{1}{72} =$

6. $\frac{1}{132} + \frac{1}{156} + \frac{1}{182} =$

7. $\frac{1}{90} + \frac{1}{110} + \frac{1}{132} =$

8. $\frac{1}{12} + \frac{1}{20} + \frac{1}{30} =$

9. $\frac{1}{110} + \frac{1}{132} + \frac{1}{156} =$

10. $\frac{1}{56} + \frac{1}{72} + \frac{1}{90} =$

WEEK 17 STRATEGY

Percentage: 2.5% of a Number

Strategy

Find the value of 2.5% of 60.

60 ÷ 2 = 30	Step 1: Divide the number by 2.
30 ÷ 2 = 15	Step 2: Divide the quotient obtained in Step 1 by 2.
15 ÷ 10 = 1.5	Step 3: Divide the quotient obtained in Step 2 by 10.

2.5% × 60 = **1.5**

Helpful Hint: Dividing the number by 4 first will eliminate one step from the strategy. (60 ÷ 4) ÷ 10 = 15 ÷ 10 = 1.5

Solve each problem mentally.

1. 2.5% of 18 =
2. 2.5% of 24 =
3. 2.5% of 42 =
4. 2.5% of 36 =
5. 2.5% of 74 =
6. 2.5% of 64 =
7. 2.5% of 88 =
8. 2.5% of 96 =
9. 2.5% of 70 =
10. 2.5% of 52 =

WEEK 18

STRATEGY

Percentage: 55% of a Number

Strategy

Find the value of 55% of 50.

50 ÷ 2 = 25   Step 1: Divide the number by 2.
25 × 11 = 275   Step 2: Multiply the quotient obtained in Step 1 by 11.
275 ÷ 10 = 27.5   Step 3: Divide the product obtained in Step 2 by 10.
55% of 50 = **27.5**

Solve each problem mentally.

1. 55% of 30 =
2. 55% of 48 =
3. 55% of 12 =
4. 55% of 64 =
5. 55% of 26 =
6. 55% of 74 =
7. 55% of 96 =
8. 55% of 82 =
9. 55% of 58 =
10. 55% of 44 =

WEEK 19

STRATEGY

Percentage: $33\frac{1}{3}\%$ of a Number

Strategy

Find the value of $33\frac{1}{3}\%$ of 120.

$120 \div 3 = 40$ ❑ Divide the whole number by the denominator.

$33\frac{1}{3}\%$ of 120 = **40**

Solve each problem mentally.

1. $33\frac{1}{3}\%$ of 150 =
2. $33\frac{1}{3}\%$ of 96 =
3. $33\frac{1}{3}\%$ of 42 =
4. $33\frac{1}{3}\%$ of 36 =
5. $33\frac{1}{3}\%$ of 75 =
6. $33\frac{1}{3}\%$ of 132 =
7. $33\frac{1}{3}\%$ of 219 =
8. $33\frac{1}{3}\%$ of 57 =
9. $33\frac{1}{3}\%$ of 168 =
10. $33\frac{1}{3}\%$ of 84 =

WEEK 20

GENERAL REVIEW 4

Solve each problem mentally.

1. 2.5% of 66 =

2. 55% of 38 =

3. $\frac{1}{182} + \frac{1}{210} + \frac{1}{240} =$

4. $33\frac{1}{3}$% of 198 =

5. 2.5% of 30 =

6. 55% of 92 =

7. $33\frac{1}{3}$% of 78 =

8. 55% of 84 =

9. $\frac{1}{210} + \frac{1}{240} + \frac{1}{272} =$

10. 2.5% of 90 =

WEEK 21

STRATEGY

Squaring Numbers from 50 to 90

Strategy

Find the value of 66^2.

Step 1: To find the last digit of the answer,

$6^2 = 3$**⑥** ❏ Square the ones digit of the number. Carry the tens digit from the result to the next step.

Step 2: To find the next-to-last-digit of the answer,

$(6 \times 6) \times 2$
$= 36 \times 2$
$= 72 + 3$
$= 7$**⑤**

❏ Multiply the ones and the tens digits of the number by 2.

❏ Add the digit carried from Step 1. Carry the tens digit from the result to the next step.

Step 3: To find the first few digits of the answer,

$6^2 = 36$
$36 + 7 =$ **㊸**

❏ Square the tens digit of the number. Add the digit carried from Step 2.

$66^2 =$ **4,356**

Solve each problem mentally.

1. $73^2 =$
2. $84^2 =$
3. $59^2 =$
4. $61^2 =$
5. $74^2 =$
6. $52^2 =$
7. $67^2 =$
8. $78^2 =$
9. $89^2 =$
10. $86^2 =$

WEEK 22
STRATEGY

Squaring Numbers from 100 to 109

Strategy

Find the value of 102^2.
Step 1: To find the last two digits of the answer,
$2^2 = $ **4**   ❑ Square the ones digit of the number.
If the result of Step 1 is a one-digit number, put a 0 in the tens place.

Step 2: To find the first few digits of the answer,
$(2 \times 2) + 100$ ❑ Multiply the ones digit of the number by 2.
$= 4 + 100$ Add 100 to the product to find the answer.
$= $ **104**

$102^2 = $ **10,404**

Solve each problem mentally.

1. $101^2 = $
2. $105^2 = $
3. $106^2 = $
4. $109^2 = $
5. $103^2 = $
6. $108^2 = $
7. $107^2 = $
8. $104^2 = $
9. $102^2 = $
10. $100^2 = $

WEEK 23
STRATEGY

Squaring: Adding the Square of a Number and its Double

Strategy

Find the value of $7^2 + 14^2$.

$7 + 7 = 14$

$7^2 = 49$

$49 \times 5 = 245$

$7^2 + 14^2 = \mathbf{245}$

Step 1: Be sure that the larger addend is a double of the smaller addend.
Step 2: Square the smaller addend.
Step 3: Multiply the result by 5 to find the answer.

Solve each problem mentally.

1. $10^2 + 20^2 =$
2. $8^2 + 16^2 =$
3. $5^2 + 10^2 =$
4. $13^2 + 26^2 =$
5. $12^2 + 24^2 =$
6. $20^2 + 40^2 =$
7. $14^2 + 28^2 =$
8. $9^2 + 18^2 =$
9. $11^2 + 22^2 =$
10. $15^2 + 30^2 =$

WEEK 24
STRATEGY

Squaring: Subtracting the Squares of Two Consecutive Numbers

Strategy

Find the value of $11^2 - 10^2$.

$10 + 0.5 = 10.5$ Step 1: Add 0.5 to the smaller number.

$10.5 \times 2 = 21$ Step 2: Multiply the result by 2 to find the answer.

$11^2 - 10^2 = \mathbf{21}$

Solve each problem mentally.

1. $21^2 - 20^2 =$

2. $43^2 - 42^2 =$

3. $14^2 - 13^2 =$

4. $38^2 - 37^2 =$

5. $62^2 - 61^2 =$

6. $85^2 - 84^2 =$

7. $90^2 - 89^2 =$

8. $49^2 - 48^2 =$

9. $77^2 - 76^2 =$

10. $69^2 - 68^2 =$

WEEK 25

GENERAL REVIEW 5

Solve each problem mentally.

1. $109^2 =$

2. $88^2 =$

3. $21^2 + 42^2 =$

4. $100^2 - 99^2 =$

5. $25^2 + 50^2 =$

6. $30^2 + 60^2 =$

7. $72^2 =$

8. $69^2 =$

9. $89^2 - 88^2 =$

10. $103^2 =$

WEEK 26

STRATEGY

Square Root: Finding the Square Root of Numbers Ending with 1

Strategy

Find the value of $\sqrt{6{,}561}$.

Step 1: To find the first digit of the answer,

$\sqrt{65} \approx \sqrt{64} = \mathbf{8}^2$

❏ Use the first two digits in the number to determine the closest lower square root whole number.

Note: If the number has three digits, determine the closest square root whole number of the first digit.
If the number has five digits, determine the closest square root whole number of the first three digits.

Step 2: The last digit of the answer is always 1.

$\sqrt{6{,}561} = \mathbf{81}$

Note: This strategy only works with three-, four-, and five-digit numbers.

Solve each problem mentally.

1. $\sqrt{5{,}041} =$

2. $\sqrt{441} =$

3. $\sqrt{1{,}681} =$

4. $\sqrt{961} =$

5. $\sqrt{10{,}201} =$

6. $\sqrt{2{,}601} =$

7. $\sqrt{8{,}281} =$

8. $\sqrt{121} =$

9. $\sqrt{3{,}721} =$

10. $\sqrt{12{,}321} =$

WEEK 27 STRATEGY

Square Root: Finding the Square Root of Numbers Ending with 5

Strategy

Find the value of $\sqrt{2{,}025}$.

Step 1: To find the first digit of the answer,

$\sqrt{20} \approx \sqrt{16} = \boxed{4}^2$

- Use the first two digits in the number to determine the closest lower square root whole number.

Note: If the number has three digits, determine the closest square root whole number of the first digit.
If the number has five digits, determine the closest square root whole number of the first three digits.

Step 2: The last digit of the answer is always 5.

$\sqrt{2{,}025} = \mathbf{45}$

Note: This strategy only works with three-, four-, and five-digit numbers.

Solve each problem mentally.

1. $\sqrt{225} =$

2. $\sqrt{5{,}625} =$

3. $\sqrt{3{,}025} =$

4. $\sqrt{9{,}025} =$

5. $\sqrt{7{,}225} =$

6. $\sqrt{4{,}225} =$

7. $\sqrt{625} =$

8. $\sqrt{13{,}225} =$

9. $\sqrt{1{,}225} =$

10. $\sqrt{11{,}025} =$

STRATEGY

Cube Root: Finding the Cube Root of Numbers Ending with 2, 3, 7, and 8

Strategy

Find the value of $\sqrt[3]{2,197}$.

Step 1: To find the first digit of the answer,

$\sqrt[3]{2} \approx \sqrt[3]{1} = \text{①}^3$

❏ Use the thousands place value digit in the number to determine the closest lower cube root whole number.

Note: If the number has five digits, determine the closest cube root whole number of the first two digits.

last digit of the number	last digit of the answer
2	8
3	7
7	3
8	2

Step 2: Refer to the table to find the last digit of the answer.

$\sqrt[3]{2,197} = 13$

Note: This strategy only works with four- and five-digit numbers.

Solve each problem mentally.

1. $\sqrt[3]{1,728} =$

2. $\sqrt[3]{10,648} =$

3. $\sqrt[3]{5,832} =$

4. $\sqrt[3]{19,683} =$

5. $\sqrt[3]{4,913} =$

6. $\sqrt[3]{2,197} =$

7. $\sqrt[3]{21,952} =$

8. $\sqrt[3]{12,167} =$

9. $\sqrt[3]{32,768} =$

10. $\sqrt[3]{54,872} =$

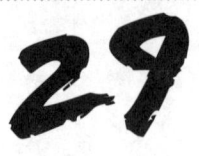

STRATEGY

Cube Root: Finding the Cube Root of Numbers Ending with 0, 1, 4, 5, 6, and 9

Strategy

Find the value of $\sqrt[3]{13{,}824}$.

Step 1: To find the first digit of the answer,

$\sqrt[3]{13} \approx \sqrt[3]{8} = \mathbf{2}^3$

☐ Use the first two digits in the number to determine the closest lower cube root whole number.

Step 2: The last digit of the number will be the last digit of the answer.

$\sqrt[3]{13{,}824} = \mathbf{24}$

Note: This strategy only works with five-digit numbers.

Solve each problem mentally.

1. $\sqrt[3]{17{,}576} =$
2. $\sqrt[3]{29{,}791} =$
3. $\sqrt[3]{46{,}656} =$
4. $\sqrt[3]{59{,}319} =$
5. $\sqrt[3]{64{,}000} =$
6. $\sqrt[3]{27{,}000} =$
7. $\sqrt[3]{42{,}875} =$
8. $\sqrt[3]{24{,}389} =$
9. $\sqrt[3]{15{,}625} =$
10. $\sqrt[3]{39{,}304} =$

WEEK 30

GENERAL REVIEW 6

Solve each problem mentally.

1. $\sqrt{14{,}641} =$

2. $\sqrt[3]{10{,}648} =$

3. $\sqrt{17{,}161} =$

4. $\sqrt[3]{29{,}791} =$

5. $\sqrt{5{,}625} =$

6. $\sqrt[3]{39{,}304} =$

7. $\sqrt{15{,}625} =$

8. $\sqrt{9{,}025} =$

9. $\sqrt[3]{74{,}088} =$

10. $\sqrt[3]{19{,}683} =$

STRATEGY

Time: Finding the Day of the Week in the 21st Century

Strategy

Find the day of the week for June 6, 2007.

$1\frac{1}{4} \times 07 = \frac{5}{4} \times 7$

$= \frac{35}{4} = 8\frac{3}{4}$

$8 + 3 + 6 = 17$

January	6	July	5
February	2	August	1
March	2	September	4
April	5	October	6
May	0	November	2
June	3	December	4

$17 \div 7 = 2$ **R3**

Sunday = 0
Monday = 1
Tuesday = 2
Wednesday = 3 …

Step 1: Multiply the last two digits of the year by $1\frac{1}{4}$. The whole number of the result is the year calculation.

Step 2: Find the sum of the year calculation, the month code, and the date day: Year calculation = 8 (whole number from Step 1); Month code = 3 (Refer to the table.); Date day = 6.

Step 3: Divide the sum obtained in Step 2 by 7.

Step 4: Find the remainder from Step 3 in the list to find the day of the week. Since the remainder is 3, the day of the week is Wednesday.

Find each day of the week mentally.

1. May 15, 2005
2. August 8, 2003
3. March 23, 2009
4. April 14, 2006
5. December 29, 2010
6. July 17, 2005
7. January 1, 2007
8. June 10, 2011
9. February 19, 2006
10. November 30, 2005

STRATEGY

Time: Finding the Day of the Week in a 21st-Century Leap Year

Strategy

Find the day of the week for February 12, 2004 (a leap year).

$1\frac{1}{4} \times 04 = \frac{5}{4} \times 4$

$= \frac{20}{4} = 5$

$5 + 2 + 12 = 19$

January	6	July	5
February	2	August	1
March	2	September	4
April	5	October	6
May	0	November	2
June	3	December	4

$19 - 1 = 18$

$18 \div 7 = 2$ **R4**

Sunday = 0
Monday = 1
Tuesday = 2
Wednesday = 3
Thursday = 4 …

Step 1: Multiply the last two digits of the year by $1\frac{1}{4}$. The result is the year calculation.

Step 2: Find the sum of the year calculation, the month code, and the date day: Year calculation = 5 (whole number from Step 1); Month code = 2 (Refer to the table.); Date day = 12.

Step 3: If the month of the date falls in January or February, subtract 1 from the sum obtained in Step 2. Divide the result by 7.

Step 4: Find the remainder from Step 3 in the list to find the day of the week. Since the remainder is 4, the day of the week is Thursday.

Find each day of the week mentally.

1. January 20, 2008
2. February 1, 2012
3. March 16, 2004
4. June 25, 2004
5. July 7, 2008
6. November 14, 2000
7. December 30, 2000
8. April 28, 2008
9. May 19, 2000
10. October 11, 2012

WEEK 33

STRATEGY

Special Number 429

Strategy

Find the value of 35 × 429.

$35 \times \frac{3}{7}$ Step 1: Multiply the first factor by $\frac{3}{7}$.

$= \frac{105}{7}$

$= 15$

0 1 5   Step 2: Put a 0 before the product obtained in Step 1 to establish the hundreds place.

35 × 429 = **15,015**   Step 3: Starting with the ten thousands place, combine the results obtained in Steps 1 and 2.

Note: This strategy only works if the number multiplied by 429 is a multiple of 7.

Solve each problem mentally.

1. 70 × 429 =
2. 49 × 429 =
3. 91 × 429 =
4. 28 × 429 =
5. 98 × 429 =
6. 7 × 429 =
7. 63 × 429 =
8. 21 × 429 =
9. 56 × 429 =
10. 42 × 429 =

WEEK 34

STRATEGY

Special Number 715

Strategy

Find the value of 42 × 715.

$42 \times \dfrac{5}{7}$

$= \dfrac{210}{7}$

$= \mathbf{30}$

Step 1: Multiply the first factor by $\dfrac{5}{7}$.

030

Step 2: Put a 0 before the product obtained in Step 1 to establish the hundreds place.

42 × 715 = **30,030**

Step 3: Starting with the ten thousands place, combine the results obtained in Steps 1 and 2.

Note: This strategy only works if the number multiplied by 715 is a multiple of 7.

Solve each problem mentally.

1. 14 × 715 =
2. 7 × 715 =
3. 21 × 715 =
4. 70 × 715 =
5. 56 × 715 =
6. 63 × 715 =
7. 35 × 715 =
8. 91 × 715 =
9. 49 × 715 =
10. 98 × 715 =

WEEK 35

GENERAL REVIEW 7

Solve each problem mentally.

1. Find the day of the week for April 26, 2006.

2. 126 × 429 =

3. Find the day of the week for January 13, 2006.

4. Find the day of the week for May 30, 2000. (leap year)

5. 112 × 715 =

6. Find the day of the week for February 6, 2007.

7. Find the day of the week for November 8, 2003.

8. Find the day of the week for December 17, 2001.

9. 119 × 429 =

10. 105 × 715 =

WEEK 36
STRATEGY

Special Number 858

Strategy

Find the value of 63 × 858.

$63 \times \frac{6}{7}$ Step 1: Multiply the first factor by $\frac{6}{7}$.

$= \frac{378}{7}$

$= 54$

054   Step 2: Put a 0 before the product obtained in Step 1 to establish the hundreds place.

63 × 858 = **54,054**   Step 3: Starting with the ten thousands place, combine the results obtained in Steps 1 and 2.

Note: This strategy only works if the number multiplied by 858 is a multiple of 7.

Solve each problem mentally.

1. 35 × 858 =
2. 28 × 858 =
3. 70 × 858 =
4. 49 × 858 =
5. 91 × 858 =
6. 77 × 858 =
7. 98 × 858 =
8. 56 × 858 =
9. 84 × 858 =
10. 105 × 858 =

WEEK 37 STRATEGY

Finding the Sum of Ascending Double Numbers

Strategy

Find the value of 5 + 10 + 20 + 40 + 80.

Step 1: Be sure that each number in the series is twice the preceding number.

80 × 2 = 160

Step 2: Multiply the largest addend by 2.

160 − 5 = 155

Step 3: Subtract the smallest addend from the product obtained in Step 2.

5 + 10 + 20 + 40 + 80 = **155**

Solve each problem mentally.

1. 8 + 16 + 32 + 64 + 128 =
2. 11 + 22 + 44 + 88 + 176 =
3. 15 + 30 + 60 + 120 + 240 =
4. 20 + 40 + 80 + 160 + 320 =
5. 25 + 50 + 100 + 200 + 400 =
6. 33 + 66 + 132 + 264 + 528 =
7. 45 + 90 + 180 + 360 + 720 =
8. 50 + 100 + 200 + 400 + 800 =
9. 55 + 110 + 220 + 440 + 880 =
10. 75 + 150 + 300 + 600 + 1,200 =

WEEK 38

STRATEGY

Finding the Sum of Ascending Triple Numbers

Strategy

Find the value of 2 + 6 + 18 + 54.

54 × 3 = 162
162 − 2 = 160

160 ÷ 2 = 80

2 + 6 + 18 + 54 = **80**

Step 1: Be sure that each number in the series is three times the preceding number.
Step 2: Multiply the largest addend by 3.
Step 3: Subtract the smallest addend from the product obtained in Step 2.
Step 4: Divide the difference obtained in Step 3 by 2.

Solve each problem mentally.

1. 3 + 9 + 27 + 81 =
2. 5 + 15 + 45 + 135 =
3. 8 + 24 + 72 + 216 =
4. 6 + 18 + 54 + 162 =
5. 4 + 12 + 36 + 108 =
6. 7 + 21 + 63 + 189 =
7. 9 + 27 + 81 + 243 =
8. 10 + 30 + 90 + 270 =
9. 12 + 36 + 108 + 324 =
10. 15 + 45 + 135 + 405 =

WEEK 39

STRATEGY

Finding the Product of any Number and 99

Strategy

Find the value of 123 × 99.

123 × 100 = 12,300

12,300 − 123 = 12,177

123 × 99 = **12,177**

Step 1: Multiply the first factor by 100.

Step 2: Subtract the first factor from the product obtained in Step 1.

Solve each problem mentally.

1. 85 × 99 =
2. 203 × 99 =
3. 196 × 99 =
4. 404 × 99 =
5. 567 × 99 =
6. 789 × 99 =
7. 294 × 99 =
8. 891 × 99 =
9. 603 × 99 =
10. 311 × 99 =

GENERAL REVIEW 8

Solve each problem mentally.

1. $1 + 3 + 5 + 7 + 9 + 11 + ... + 35 =$

2. $10{,}478 \times 11 =$

3. 55% of $72 =$

4. $49 \times 59 =$

5. $\sqrt{5{,}041} =$

6. $88 \times 111 =$

7. $56^2 =$

8. $89 \times 125 =$

9. 2.5% of $48 =$

10. $108 \times 109 =$

GENERAL REVIEW 9

Solve each problem mentally.

1. 42 × 858 =

2. 2 + 4 + 6 + 8 + 10 + ... + 90 =

3. 68^2 =

4. 79 × 49 =

5. $\sqrt[3]{24{,}389}$ =

6. Find the day of the week for March 19, 2003.

7. 49 × 858 =

8. 104 × 125 =

9. 36,917 × 11 =

10. 9 + 18 + 36 + 72 + 144 =

GENERAL REVIEW 10

Solve each problem mentally.

1. $109 \times 110 =$

2. $84 \times 1\frac{1}{6} =$

3. $108^2 =$

4. $17^2 + 34^2 =$

5. $105 \times 429 =$

6. $38 + 39 + 40 + 41 + 42 + \ldots + 72 =$

7. $\frac{1}{182} + \frac{1}{210} + \frac{1}{240} =$

8. $33\frac{1}{3}\%$ of $360 =$

9. $\sqrt[3]{85,184} =$

10. Find the day of the week for January 31, 2000. (leap year)

WEEK 43

GENERAL REVIEW 11

Solve each problem mentally.

1. $\sqrt{15{,}625} =$

2. $105 \times 715 =$

3. $120 \times 125 =$

4. $88 \times 1\frac{1}{4} =$

5. $25 \times 111 =$

6. $72 \div 1\frac{1}{3} =$

7. 55% of $56 =$

8. $81^2 =$

9. $61^2 - 60^2 =$

10. $\sqrt[3]{10{,}648} =$

WEEK 44

GENERAL REVIEW 12

Solve each problem mentally.

1. 2.5% of 68 =

2. 72^2 =

3. 112^2 =

4. 1 + 3 + 5 + 7 + 9 + 11 + ... + 29 =

5. 56 × 125

6. $54 \div 1\frac{1}{2}$ =

7. $33\frac{1}{3}$% of 96 =

8. $\sqrt{8,281}$ =

9. Find the day of the week for February 17, 2005.

10. 84 × 715 =

WEEK 45

GENERAL REVIEW 13

Solve each problem mentally.

1. $79 \times 39 =$

2. $64 \times 125 =$

3. $112 \times 715 =$

4. $19^2 + 38^2 =$

5. $505 \times 99 =$

6. $35 \times 858 =$

7. $15{,}873 \times 11 =$

8. $2 + 4 + 6 + 8 + 10 + \ldots + 56 =$

9. 64^2

10. $22 + 24 + 26 + 28 + 30 =$

WEEK 46

GENERAL REVIEW 14

Solve each problem mentally.

1. $60 \times 125 =$

2. $95 \times 1\frac{1}{5} =$

3. $62^2 - 61^2 =$

4. $725 \times 99 =$

5. $69 \times 111 =$

6. $\sqrt[3]{17{,}576} =$

7. $1 + 3 + 5 + 7 + 9 + 11 + \ldots + 93 =$

8. Find the day of the week for April 13, 2004. (leap year)

9. $133 \times 429 =$

10. $44 \div 1\frac{1}{3} =$

WEEK 47

GENERAL REVIEW 15

Solve each problem mentally.

1. $24^2 + 48^2 =$

2. $28 \times 715 =$

3. $\sqrt{5,041} =$

4. $39 \times 89 =$

5. $20 + 60 + 180 + 540 + 1,620 =$

6. $38,780 \times 11 =$

7. $546 \times 99 =$

8. $39 \times 1\frac{1}{2} =$

9. 2.5% of $96 =$

10. 104×125

WEEK 48

GENERAL REVIEW 16

Solve each problem mentally.

1. $87 \times 111 =$

2. $76 \times 1\frac{1}{4} =$

3. $105 \times 106 =$

4. $147 \times 429 =$

5. $45 + 47 + 49 + 51 + 53 =$

6. $11 + 33 + 99 + 297 + 891 =$

7. $69 \times 29 =$

8. $54^2 =$

9. Find the day of the week for May 19, 2001.

10. $\sqrt[3]{91,125} =$

WEEK 49

GENERAL REVIEW 17

Solve each problem mentally.

1. 28 × 858 =

2. 75 × 111 =

3. 96 × $1\frac{1}{3}$ =

4. 98 × 99 =

5. $\sqrt{6,561}$ =

6. 35 × 429 =

7. 55% of 82 =

8. 1 + 3 + 5 + 7 + 9 + 11 + ... + 75 =

9. 15 + 30 + 60 + 120 + 240 =

10. Find the day of the week for June 21, 2000. (leap year)

WEEK 50

GENERAL REVIEW 18

Solve each problem mentally.

1. $64 \div 1\frac{1}{3} =$

2. $88^2 =$

3. $\sqrt{17,161} =$

4. $\sqrt[3]{42,875} =$

5. $347 \times 99 =$

6. $49 \times 111 =$

7. $33\frac{1}{3}\%$ of $174 =$

8. $182 \times 429 =$

9. $21^2 - 20^2 =$

10. $17 + 18 + 19 + 20 + 21 + \ldots + 54 =$

WEEK 51

GENERAL REVIEW 19

Solve each problem mentally.

1. $29 \times 111 =$

2. 2.5% of $160 =$

3. $109^2 =$

4. $25^2 + 50^2 =$

5. $97 \times 98 =$

6. $45 + 90 + 180 + 360 + 720 =$

7. $\sqrt[3]{21{,}952} =$

8. $21 \times 858 =$

9. Find the day of the week for December 9, 2005.

10. $16 + 48 + 144 + 432 + 1{,}296 =$

WEEK 52

GENERAL REVIEW 20

Solve each problem mentally.

1. 403×99

2. $14 \times 715 =$

3. $\sqrt{3{,}025} =$

4. $59 \times 99 =$

5. $30{,}157 \times 11 =$

6. $48 \times 1\frac{1}{3} =$

7. $49^2 =$

8. $\sqrt[3]{64{,}000} =$

9. $58^2 - 57^2 =$

10. $36 + 38 + 40 + 42 + 44 + 46 + 48 =$

Notes

ANSWER KEY — Mental Math Level 6

WEEK 1
1. 400
2. 81
3. 729
4. 576
5. 169
6. 1,681
7. 1,600
8. 1,089
9. 2,209
10. 225

WEEK 2
1. 1,892
2. 2,450
3. 182
4. 506
5. 1,122
6. 650
7. 272
8. 1,406
9. 90
10. 702

WEEK 3
1. 3,195
2. 715
3. 1,395
4. 779
5. 2,250
6. 1,659
7. 1,705
8. 2,940
9. 1,209
10. 3,975

WEEK 4
1. 120
2. 90
3. 195
4. 315
5. 371
6. 504
7. 742
8. 1,078
9. 702
10. 1,782

WEEK 5
1. 2,500
2. 420
3. 1,725
4. 380
5. 306
6. 1,127
7. 882
8. 846
9. 3,600
10. 2,889

WEEK 6
1. 1,421
2. 1,131
3. 3,381
4. 1,121
5. 6,141
6. 3,081
7. 7,031
8. 9,801
9. 931
10. 3,861

WEEK 7
1. 2,442
2. 5,106
3. 4,329
4. 7,104
5. 9,990
6. 7,992
7. 6,105
8. 8,991
9. 8,769
10. 1,887

WEEK 8
1. 9,000
2. 10,500
3. 6,000
4. 7,000
5. 8,000
6. 12,000
7. 3,500
8. 6,500
9. 2,000
10. 5,000

WEEK 9
1. 451,396
2. 895,763
3. 1,019,678
4. 618,684
5. 202,587
6. 381,689
7. 680,372
8. 805,398
9. 265,837
10. 554,169

WEEK 10
1. 5,841
2. 4,884
3. 6,241
4. 2,581
5. 4,107
6. 472,296
7. 8,500
8. 397,397
9. 2,500
10. 266,167

WEEK 11
1. 8,742
2. 9,702
3. 9,120
4. 8,372
5. 9,506
6. 8,930
7. 8,556
8. 9,900
9. 9,312
10. 8,190

WEEK 12
1. 10,920
2. 11,342
3. 10,302
4. 11,556
5. 10,712
6. 10,100
7. 11,990
8. 10,506
9. 11,772
10. 11,130

© Singapore Asian Publications (S) Pte Ltd

WEEK 13
1. 40
2. $34\frac{4}{5}$
3. 56
4. $26\frac{1}{4}$
5. 105
6. $109\frac{1}{2}$
7. $61\frac{1}{9}$
8. 66
9. $100\frac{4}{5}$
10. 132

WEEK 14
1. 21
2. 27
3. 36
4. 45
5. 63
6. 64
7. 26
8. 72
9. 75
10. 72

WEEK 15
1. 11,556
2. $18\frac{2}{7}$
3. 8,930
4. 76
5. 72
6. 65
7. 15
8. 120
9. 8,372
10. 11,342

WEEK 16
1. $\frac{3}{10}$
2. $\frac{3}{40}$
3. $\frac{3}{180}$
4. $\frac{3}{88}$
5. $\frac{3}{54}$
6. $\frac{3}{154}$
7. $\frac{3}{108}$
8. $\frac{3}{18}$
9. $\frac{3}{130}$
10. $\frac{3}{70}$

WEEK 17
1. 0.45
2. 0.6
3. 1.05
4. 0.9
5. 1.85
6. 1.6
7. 2.2
8. 2.4
9. 1.75
10. 1.3

WEEK 18
1. 16.5
2. 26.4
3. 6.6
4. 35.2
5. 14.3
6. 40.7
7. 52.8
8. 45.1
9. 31.9
10. 24.2

WEEK 19
1. 50
2. 32
3. 14
4. 12
5. 25
6. 44
7. 73
8. 19
9. 56
10. 28

WEEK 20
1. 1.65
2. 20.9
3. $\frac{3}{208}$
4. 66
5. 0.75
6. 50.6
7. 26
8. 46.2
9. $\frac{3}{238}$
10. 2.25

WEEK 21
1. 5,329
2. 7,056
3. 3,481
4. 3,721
5. 5,476
6. 2,704
7. 4,489
8. 6,084
9. 7,921
10. 7,396

WEEK 22
1. 10,201
2. 11,025
3. 11,236
4. 11,881
5. 10,609
6. 11,664
7. 11,449
8. 10,816
9. 10,404
10. 10,000

WEEK 23
1. 500
2. 320
3. 125
4. 845
5. 720
6. 2,000
7. 980
8. 405
9. 605
10. 1,125

WEEK 24
1. 41
2. 85
3. 27
4. 75
5. 123
6. 169
7. 179
8. 97
9. 153
10. 137

Week 25
1. 11,881
2. 7,744
3. 2,205
4. 199
5. 3,125
6. 4,500
7. 5,184
8. 4,761
9. 177
10. 10,609

Week 26
1. 71
2. 21
3. 41
4. 31
5. 101
6. 51
7. 91
8. 11
9. 61
10. 111

Week 27
1. 15
2. 75
3. 55
4. 95
5. 85
6. 65
7. 25
8. 115
9. 35
10. 105

Week 28
1. 12
2. 22
3. 18
4. 27
5. 17
6. 13
7. 28
8. 23
9. 32
10. 38

Week 29
1. 26
2. 31
3. 36
4. 39
5. 40
6. 30
7. 35
8. 29
9. 25
10. 34

Week 30
1. 121
2. 22
3. 131
4. 31
5. 75
6. 34
7. 125
8. 95
9. 42
10. 27

Week 31
1. Sunday
2. Friday
3. Monday
4. Friday
5. Wednesday
6. Sunday
7. Monday
8. Friday
9. Sunday
10. Wednesday

Week 32
1. Sunday
2. Wednesday
3. Tuesday
4. Friday
5. Monday
6. Tuesday
7. Saturday
8. Monday
9. Friday
10. Thursday

Week 33
1. 30,030
2. 21,021
3. 39,039
4. 12,012
5. 42,042
6. 3,003
7. 27,027
8. 9,009
9. 24,024
10. 18,018

Week 34
1. 10,010
2. 5,005
3. 15,015
4. 50,050
5. 40,040
6. 45,045
7. 25,025
8. 65,065
9. 35,035
10. 70,070

Week 35
1. Wednesday
2. 54,054
3. Friday
4. Tuesday
5. 80,080
6. Tuesday
7. Saturday
8. Monday
9. 51,051
10. 75,075

Week 36
1. 30,030
2. 24,024
3. 60,060
4. 42,042
5. 78,078
6. 66,066
7. 84,084
8. 48,048
9. 72,072
10. 90,090

Week 37
1. 248
2. 341
3. 465
4. 620
5. 775
6. 1,023
7. 1,395
8. 1,550
9. 1,705
10. 2,325

Week 38
1. 120
2. 200
3. 320
4. 240
5. 160
6. 280
7. 360
8. 400
9. 480
10. 600

Week 39
1. 8,415
2. 20,097
3. 19,404
4. 39,996
5. 56,133
6. 78,111
7. 29,106
8. 88,209
9. 59,697
10. 30,789

Week 40
1. 324
2. 115,258
3. 39.6
4. 2,891
5. 71
6. 9,768
7. 3,136
8. 11,125
9. 1.2
10. 11,772

Week 41
1. 36,036
2. 2,070
3. 4,624
4. 3,871
5. 29
6. Wednesday
7. 42,042
8. 13,000
9. 406,087
10. 279

Week 42
1. 11,990
2. 98
3. 11,664
4. 1,445
5. 45,045
6. 1,925
7. $\frac{3}{208}$
8. 120
9. 44
10. Monday

Week 43
1. 125
2. 75,075
3. 15,000
4. 110
5. 2,775
6. 54
7. 30.8
8. 6,561
9. 121
10. 22

Week 44
1. 1.7
2. 5,184
3. 12,544
4. 225
5. 7,000
6. 36
7. 32
8. 91
9. Thursday
10. 60,060

Week 45
1. 3,081
2. 8,000
3. 80,080
4. 1,805
5. 49,995
6. 30,030
7. 174,603
8. 812
9. 4,096
10. 130

Week 46
1. 7,500
2. 114
3. 123
4. 71,775
5. 7,659
6. 26
7. 2,209
8. Tuesday
9. 57,057
10. 33

Week 47
1. 2,880
2. 20,020
3. 71
4. 3,471
5. 2,420
6. 426,580
7. 54,054
8. $58\frac{1}{2}$
9. 2.4
10. 13,000

Week 48
1. 9,657
2. 95
3. 11,130
4. 63,063
5. 245
6. 1,331
7. 2,001
8. 2,916
9. Saturday
10. 45

Week 49
1. 24,024
2. 8,325
3. 128
4. 9,702
5. 81
6. 15,015
7. 45.1
8. 1,444
9. 465
10. Wednesday

Week 50
1. 48
2. 7,744
3. 131
4. 35
5. 34,353
6. 5,439
7. 58
8. 78,078
9. 41
10. 1,349

Week 51
1. 3,219
2. 4
3. 11,881
4. 3,125
5. 9,506
6. 1,395
7. 28
8. 18,018
9. Friday
10. 1,936

Week 52
1. 39,897
2. 10,010
3. 55
4. 5,841
5. 331,727
6. 64
7. 2,401
8. 40
9. 115
10. 294